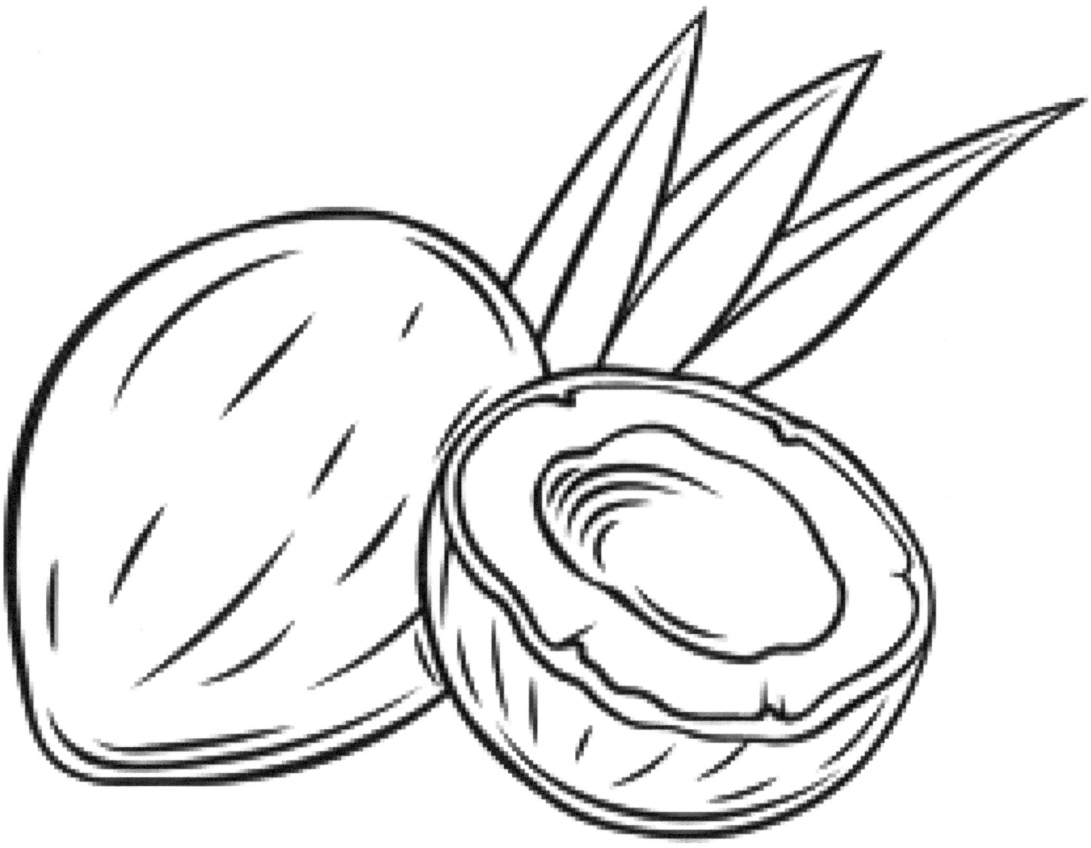

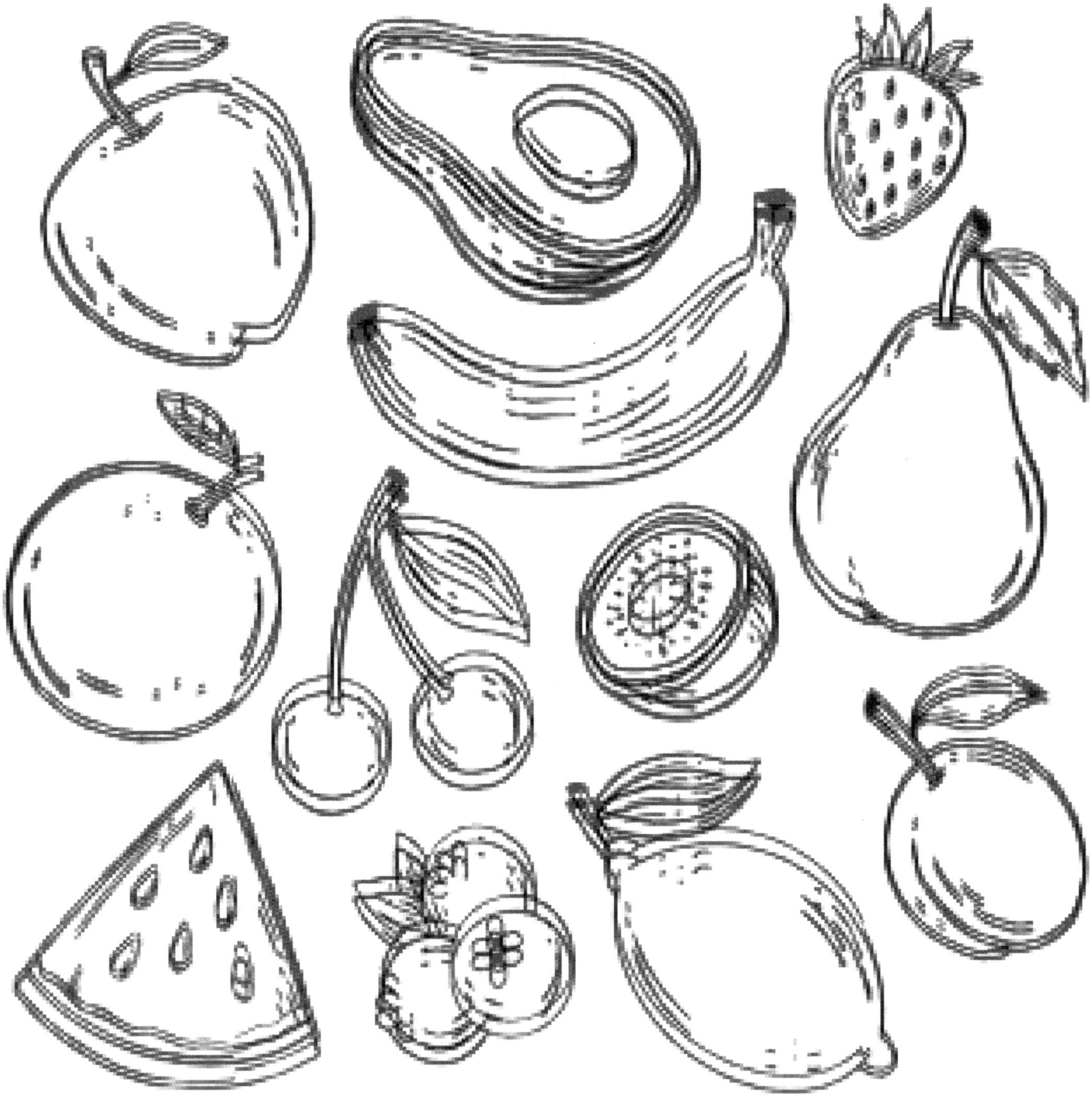

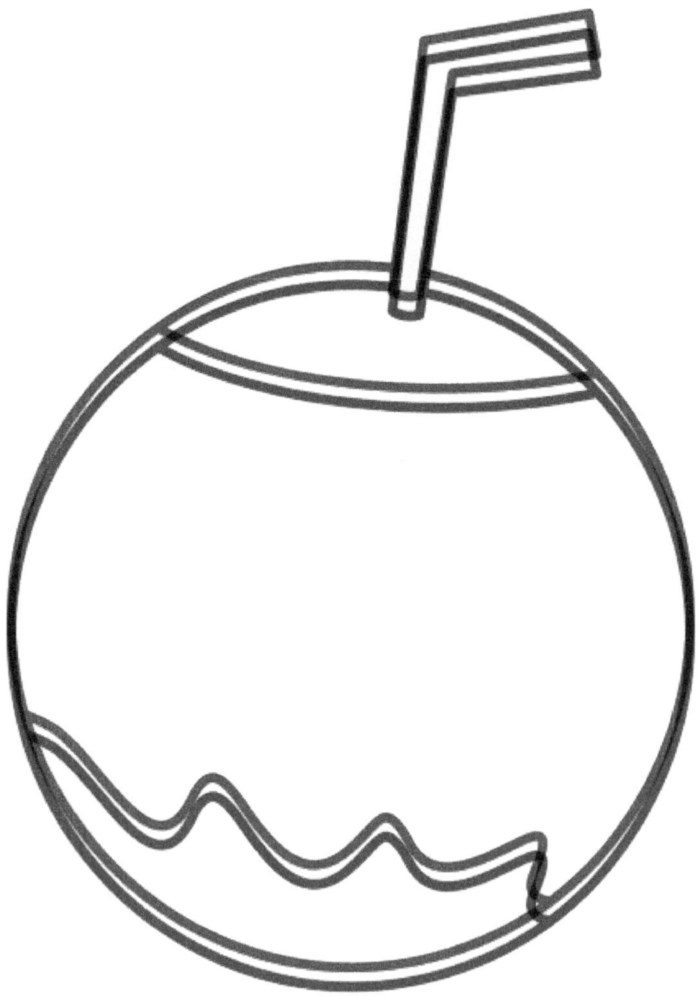

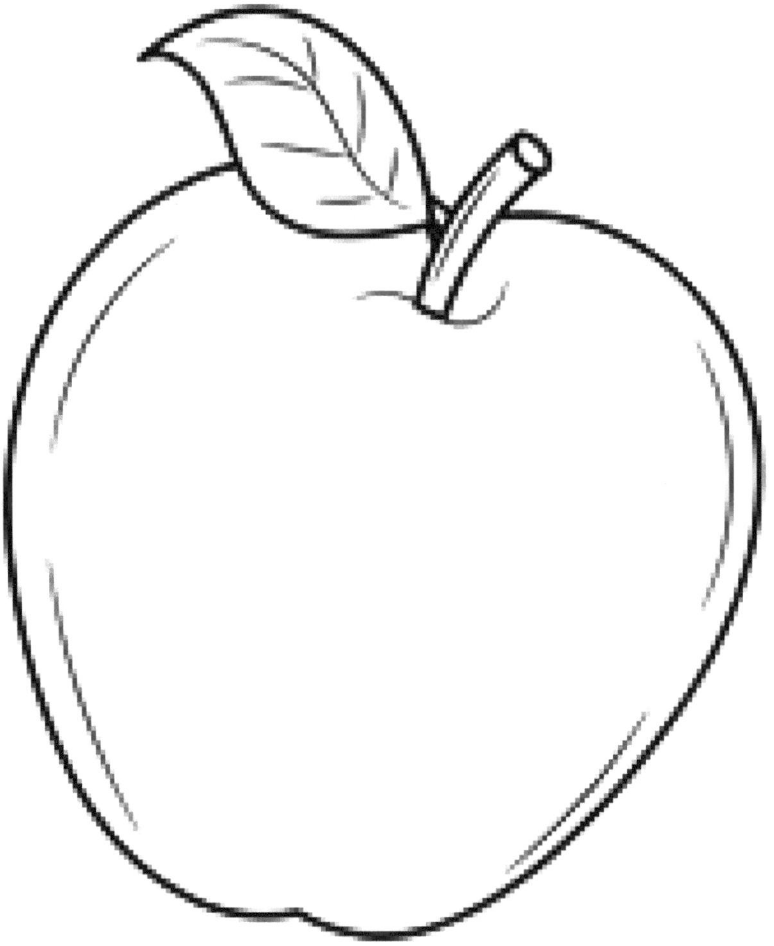

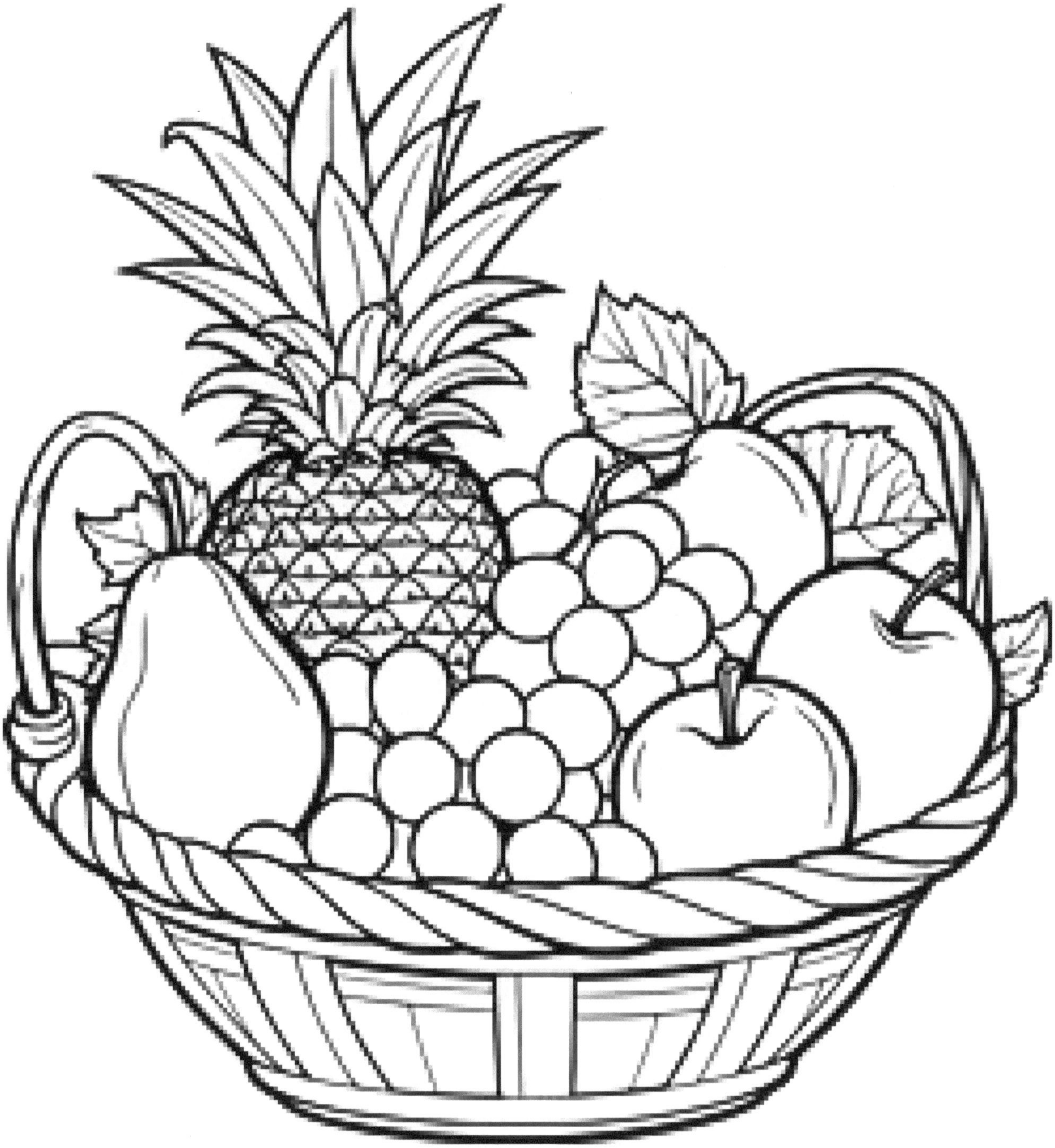

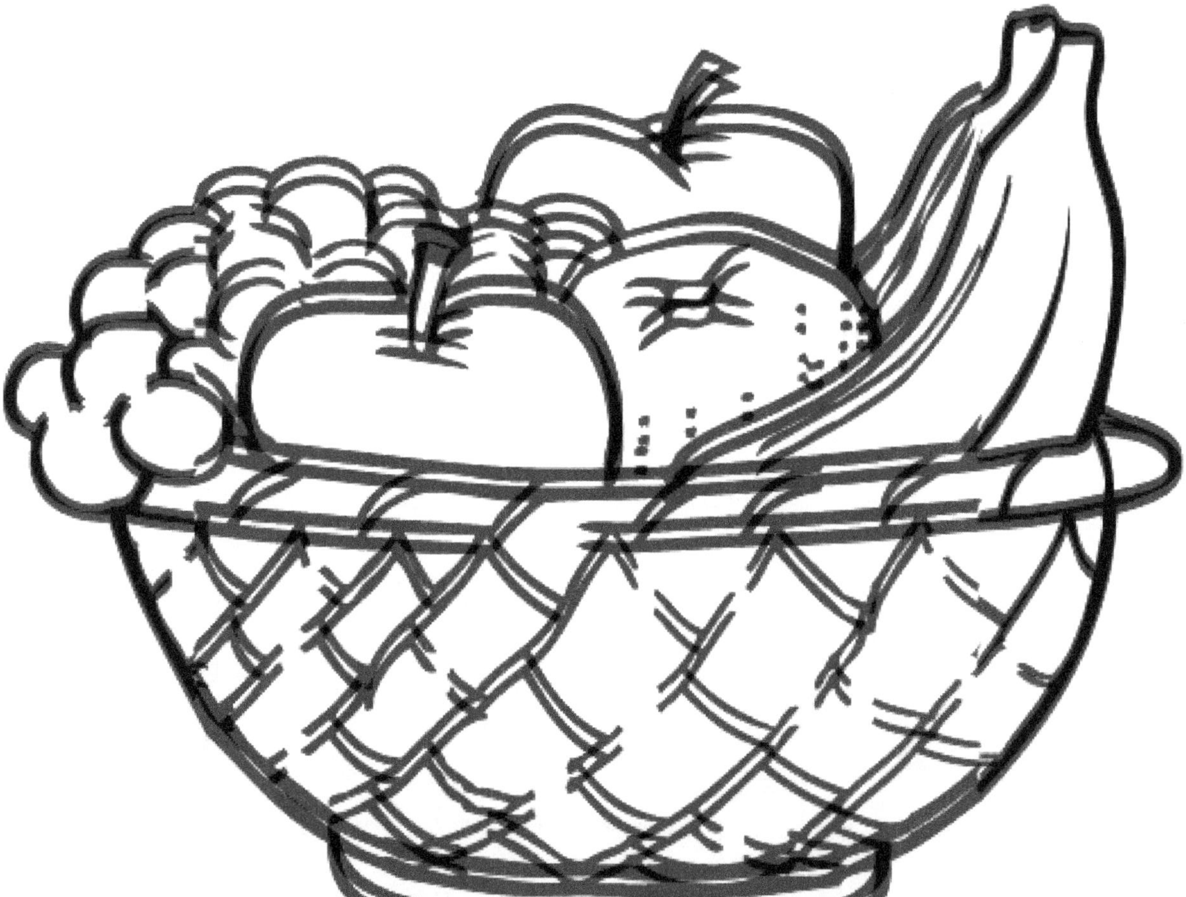

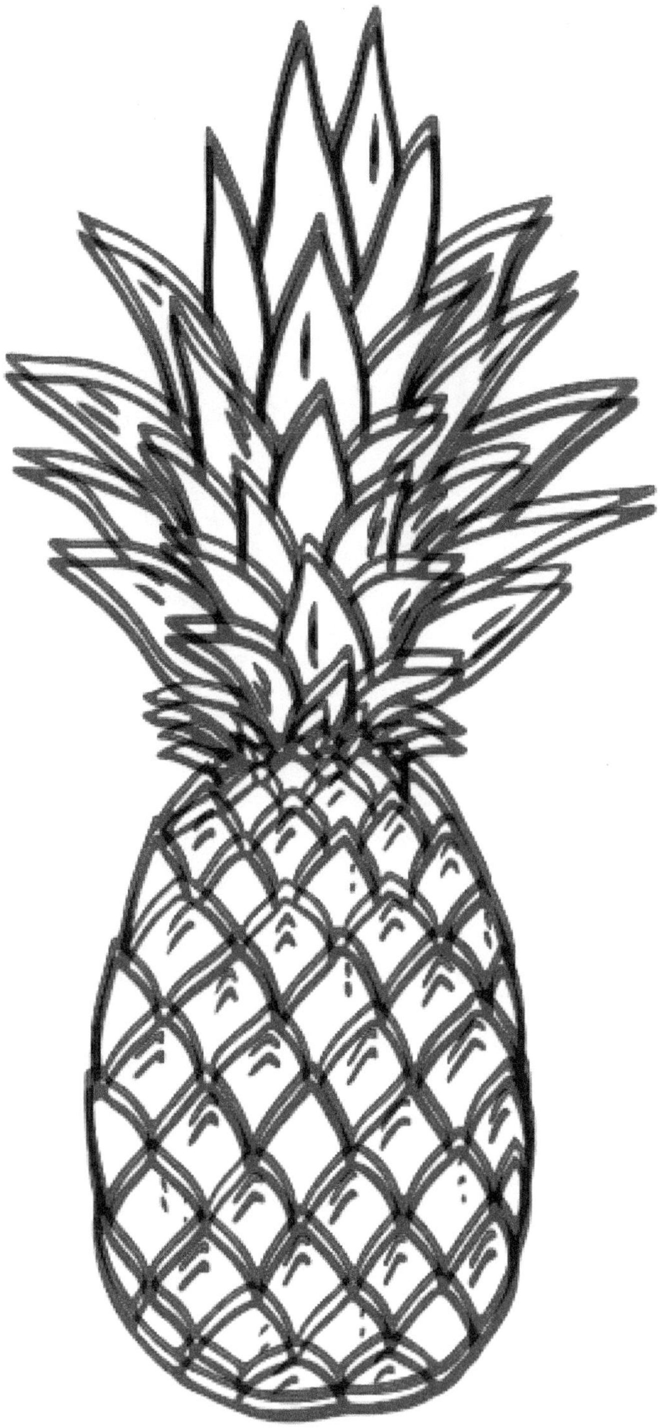

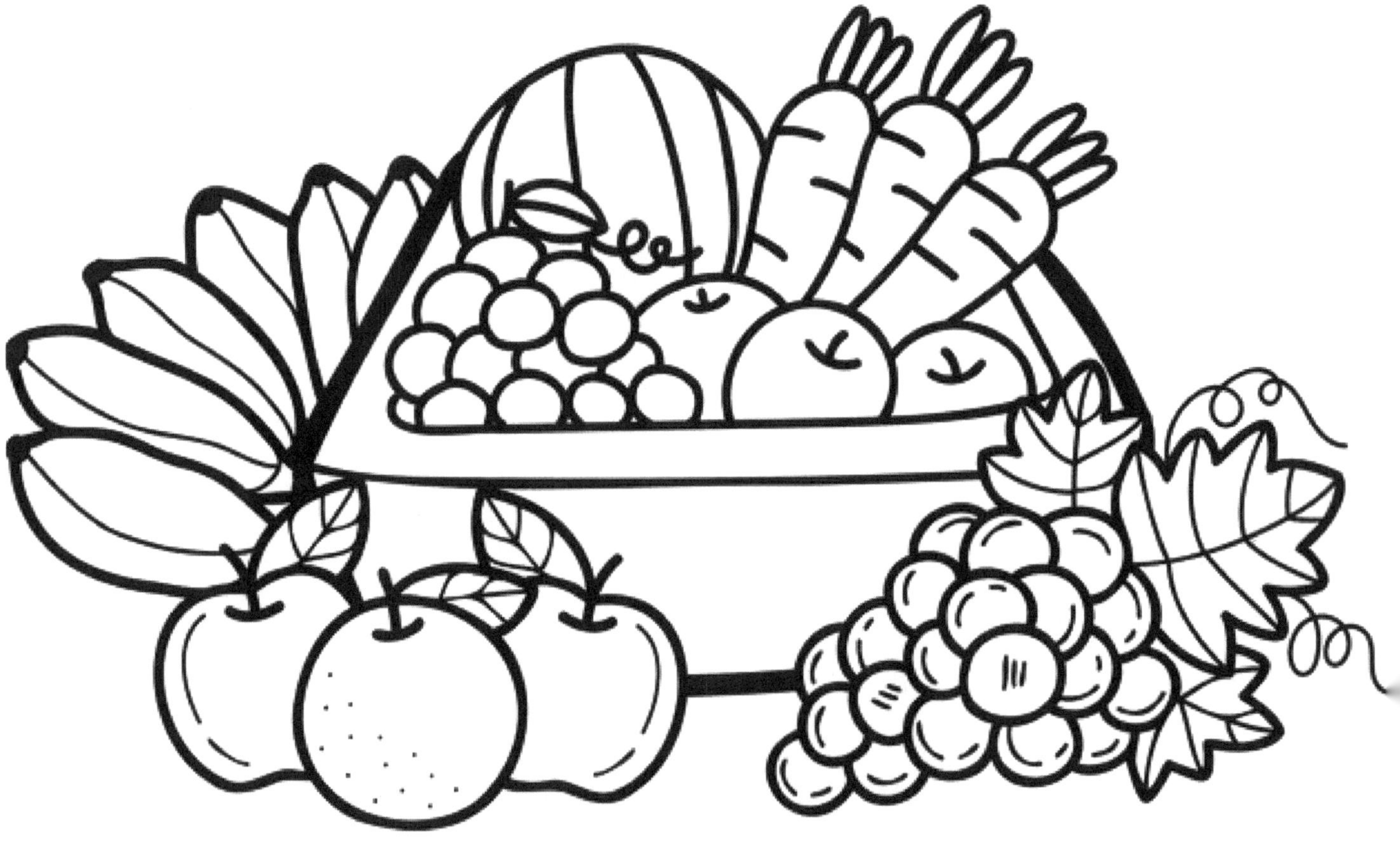

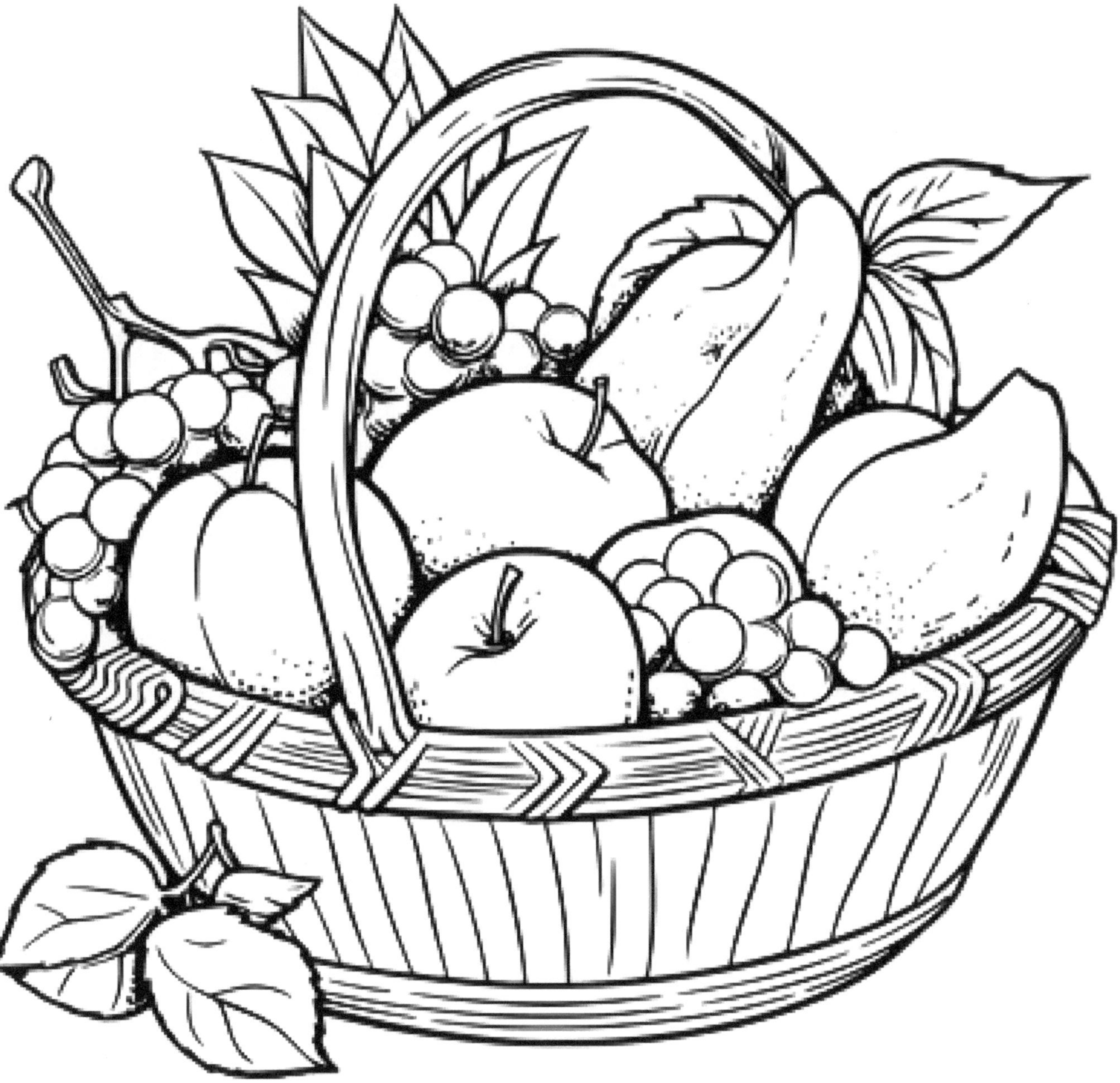

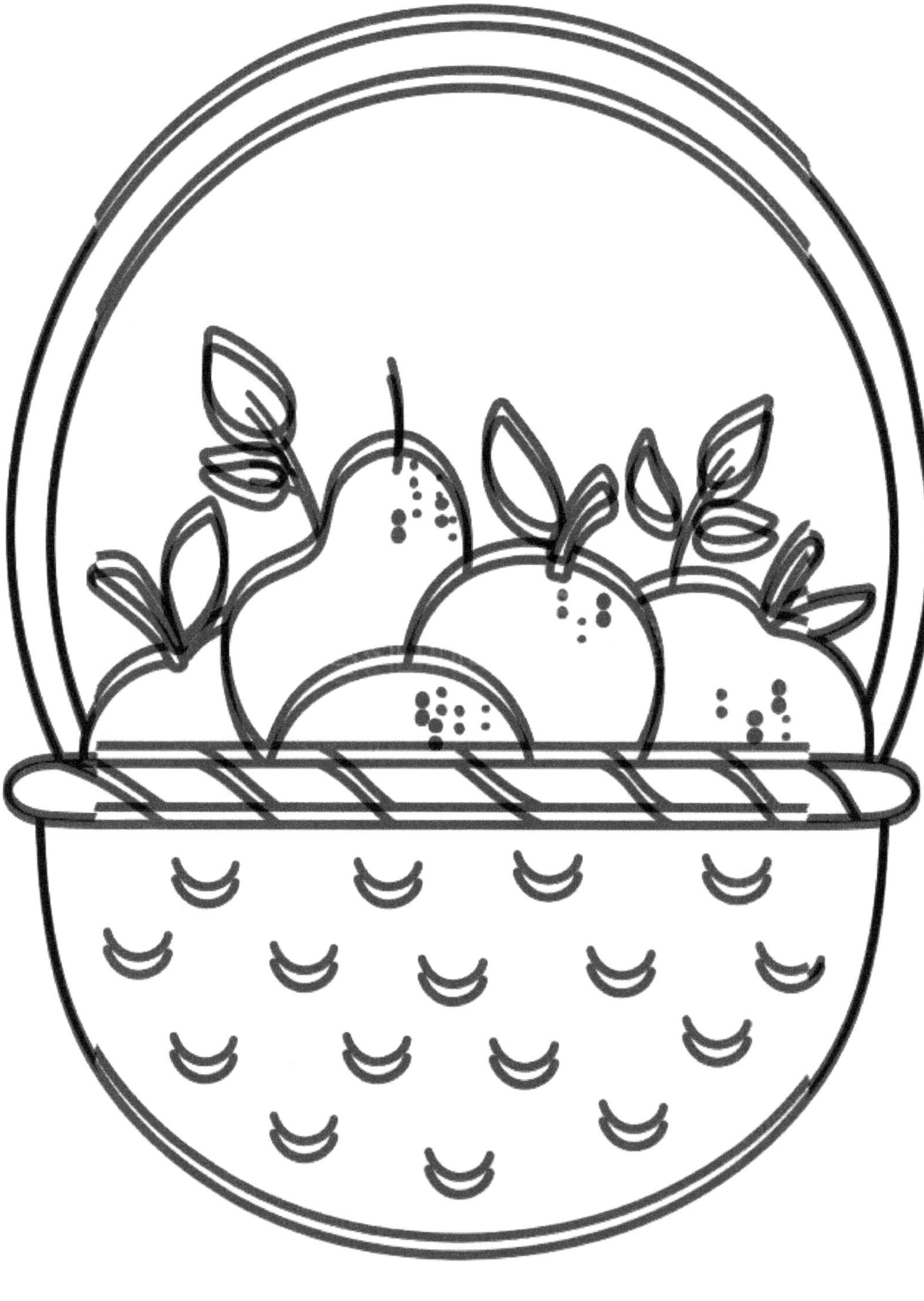

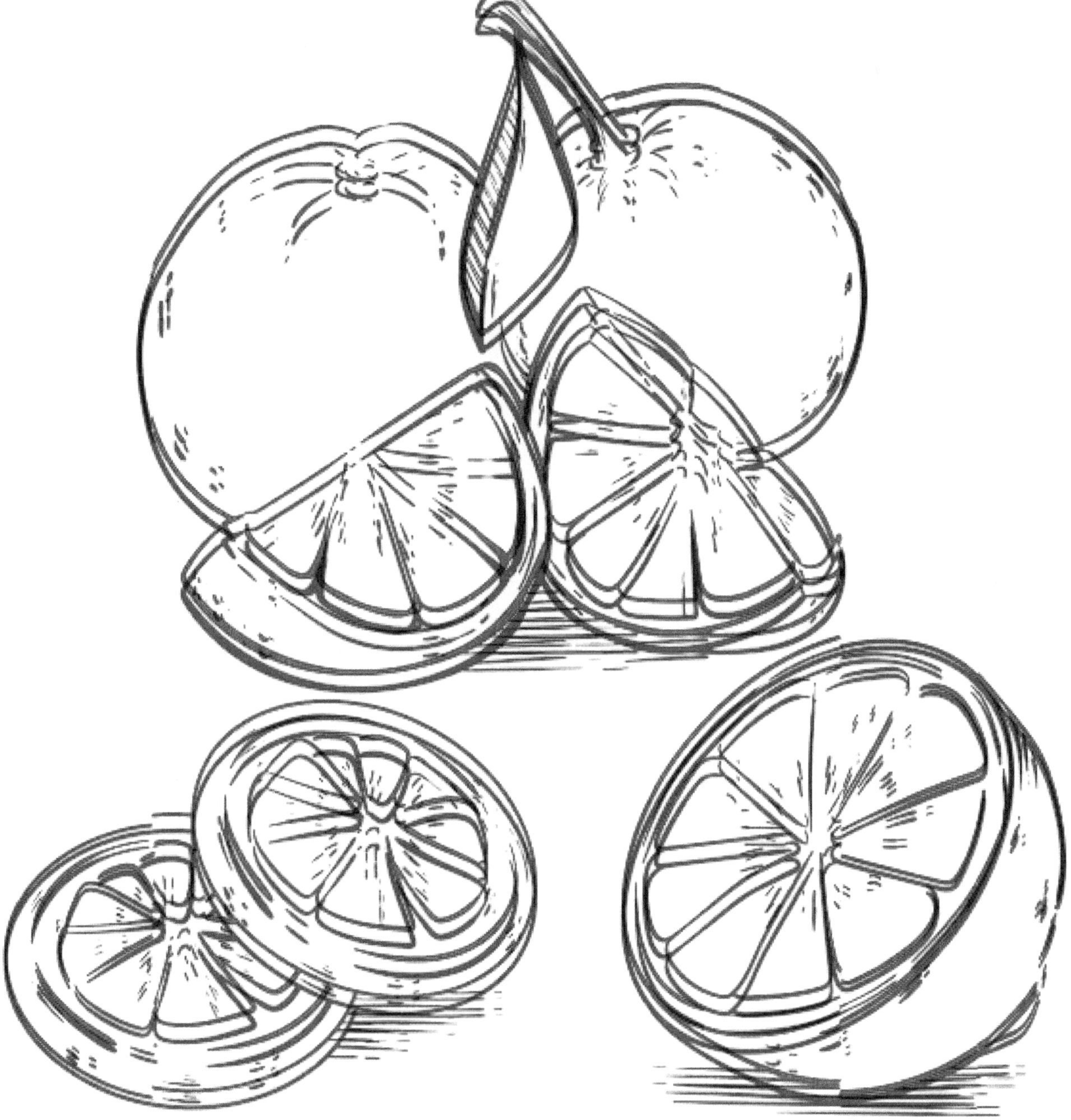

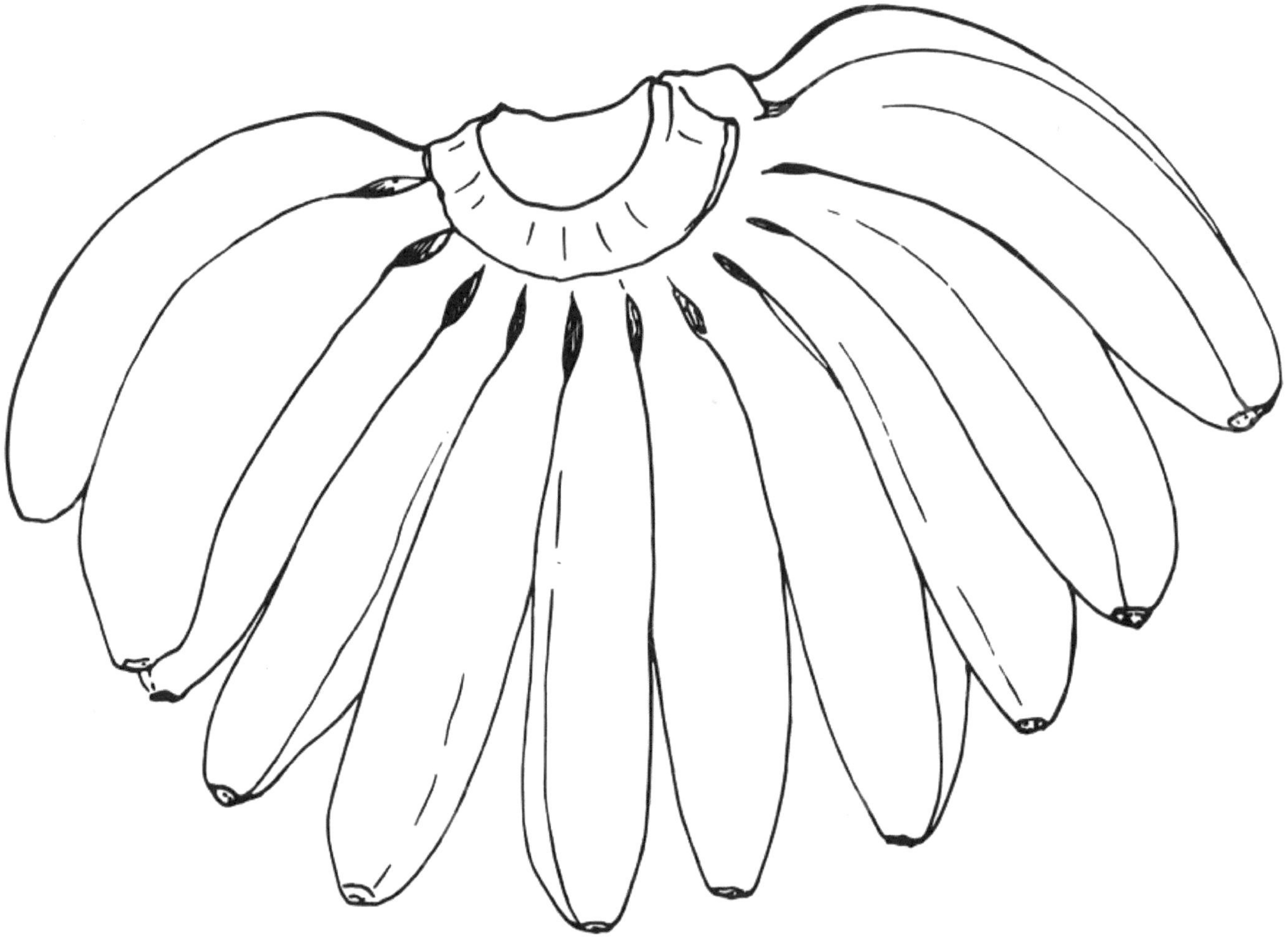

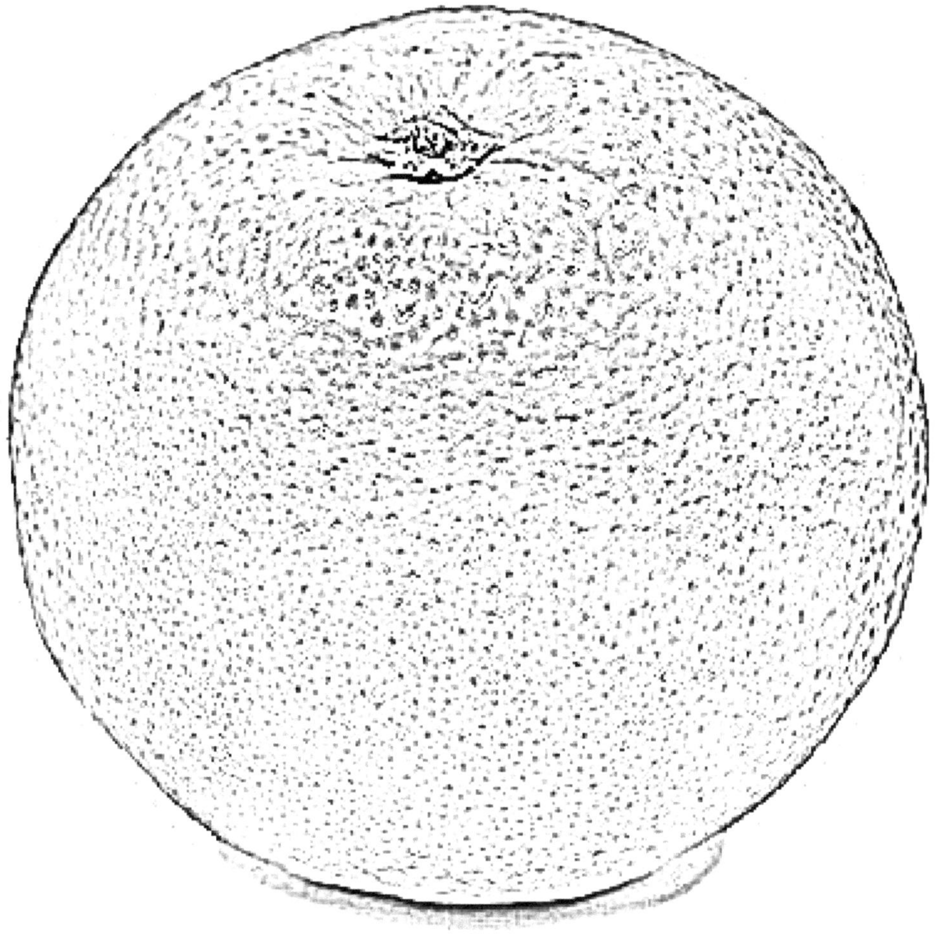

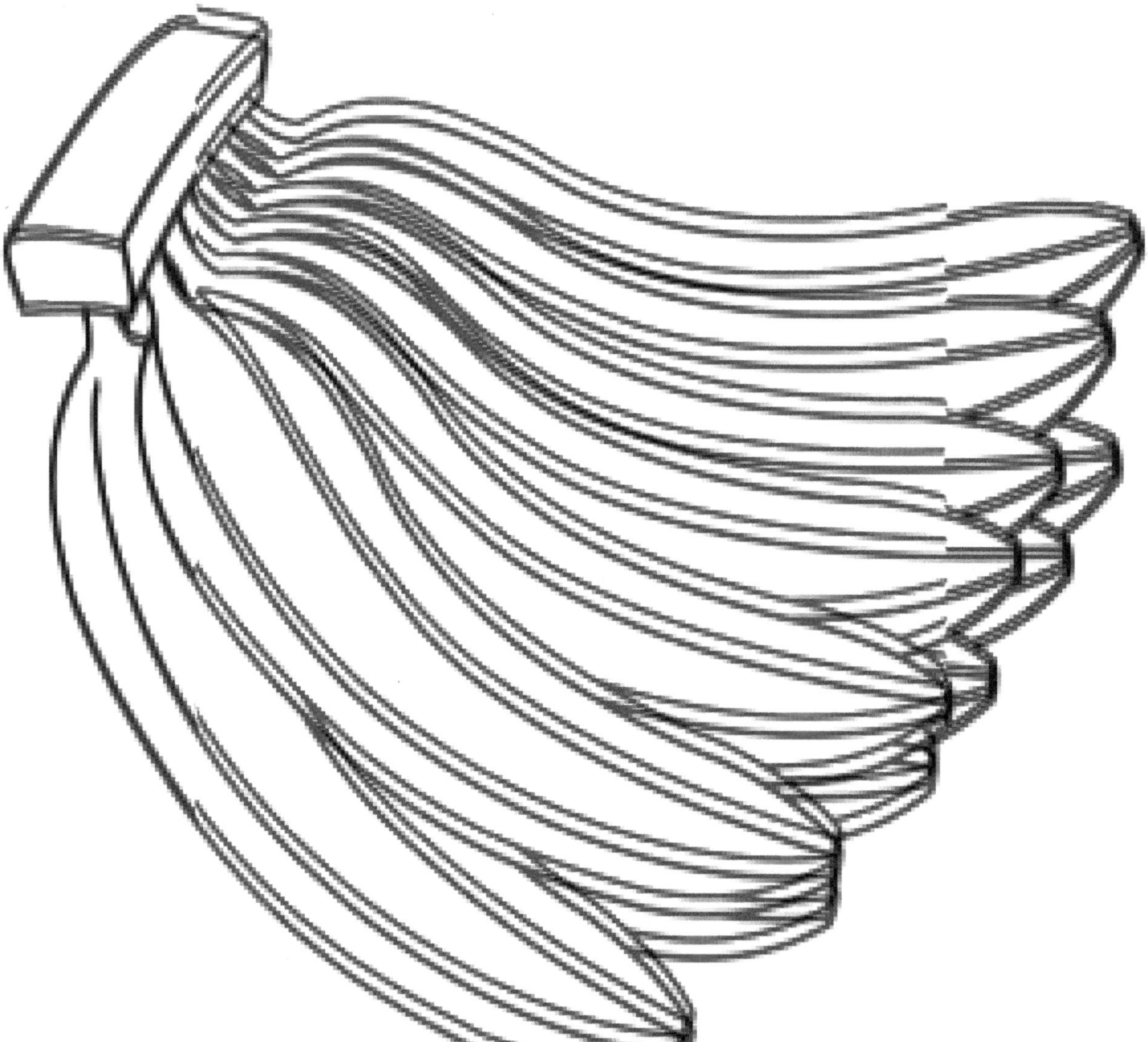

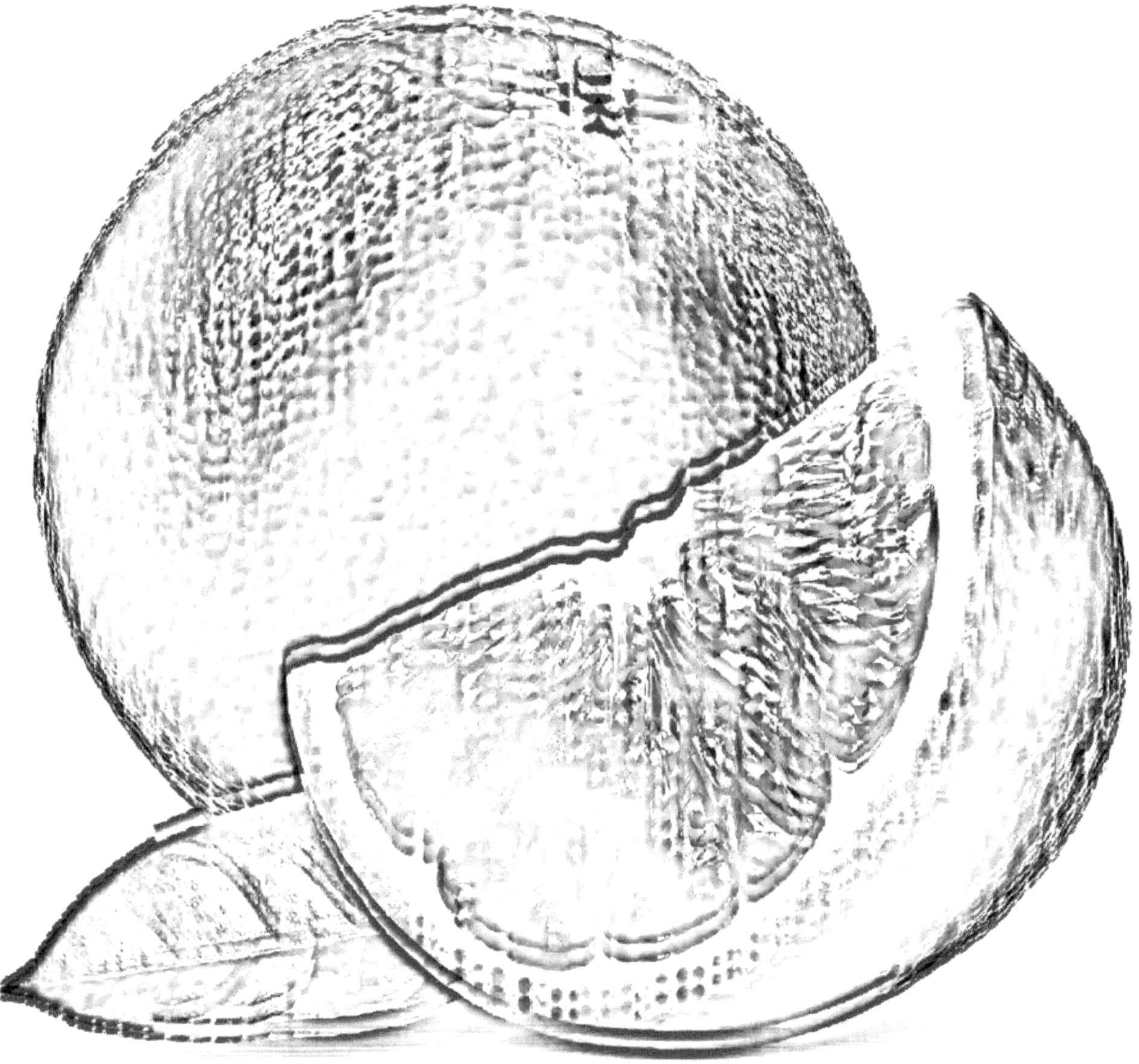

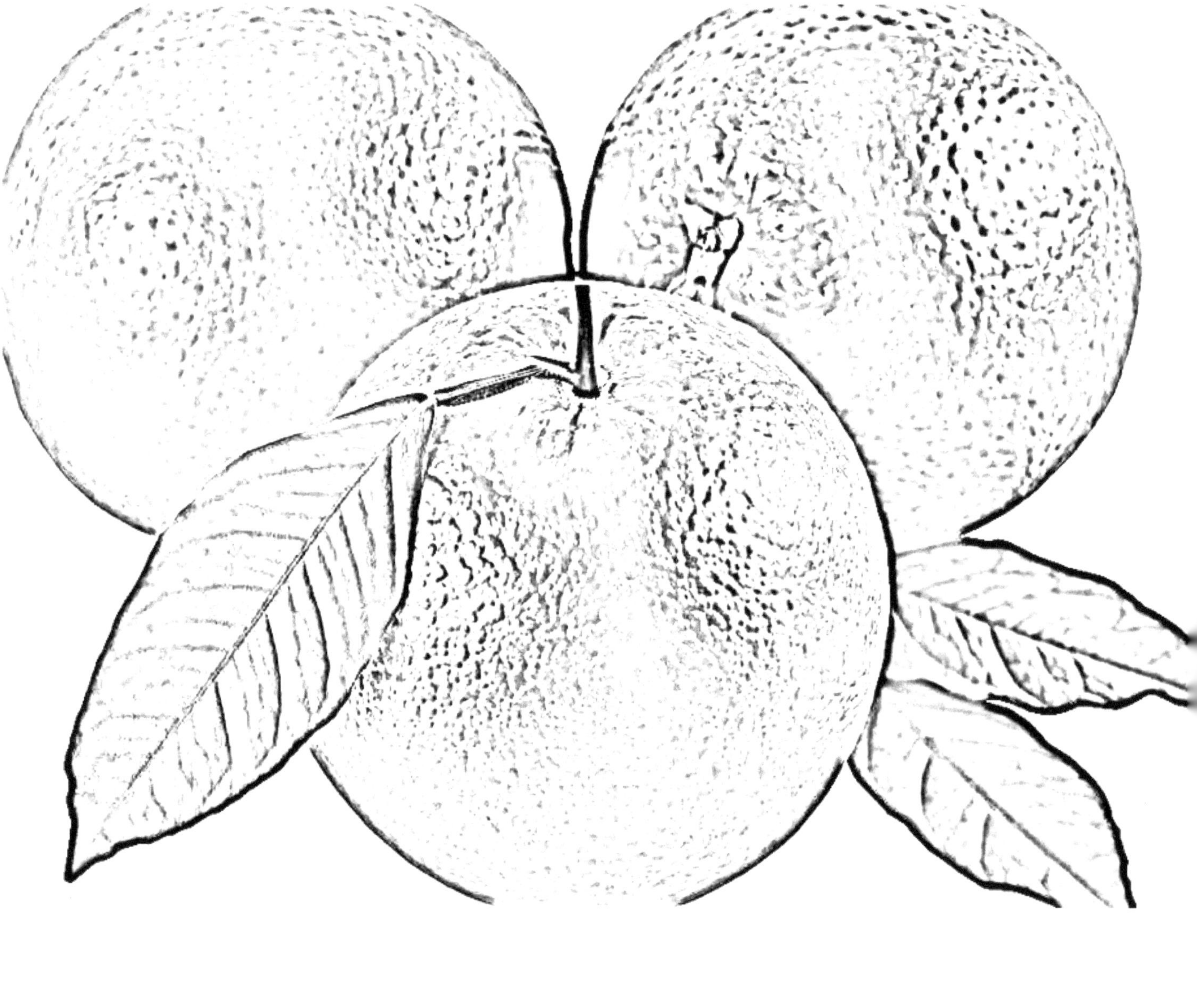

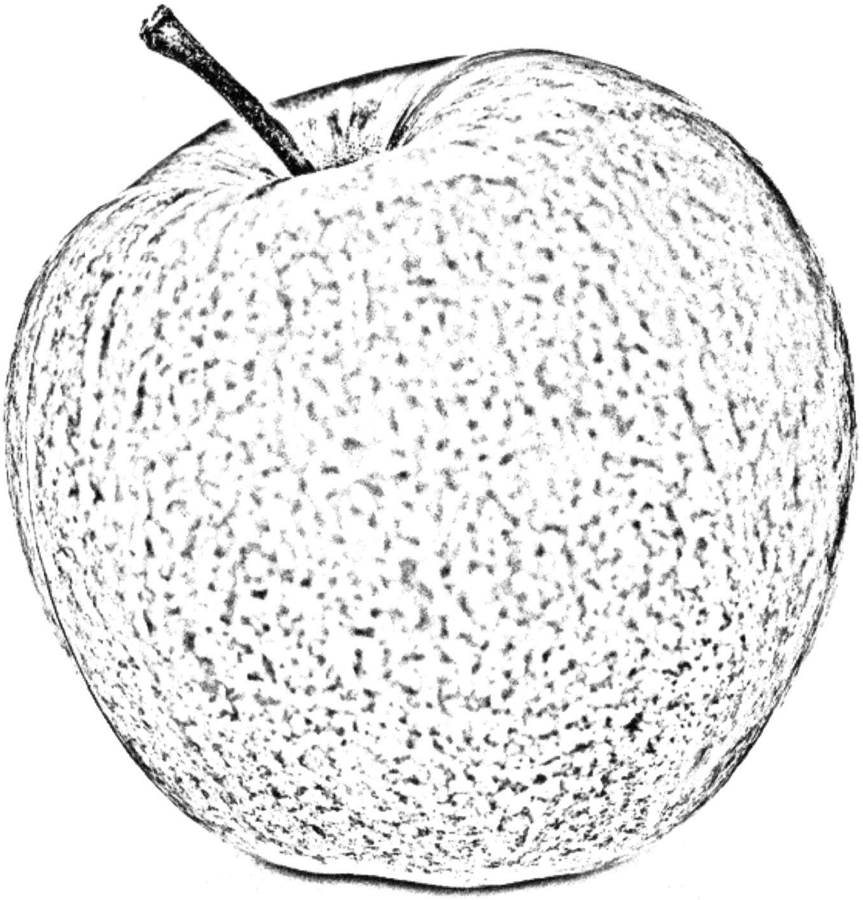

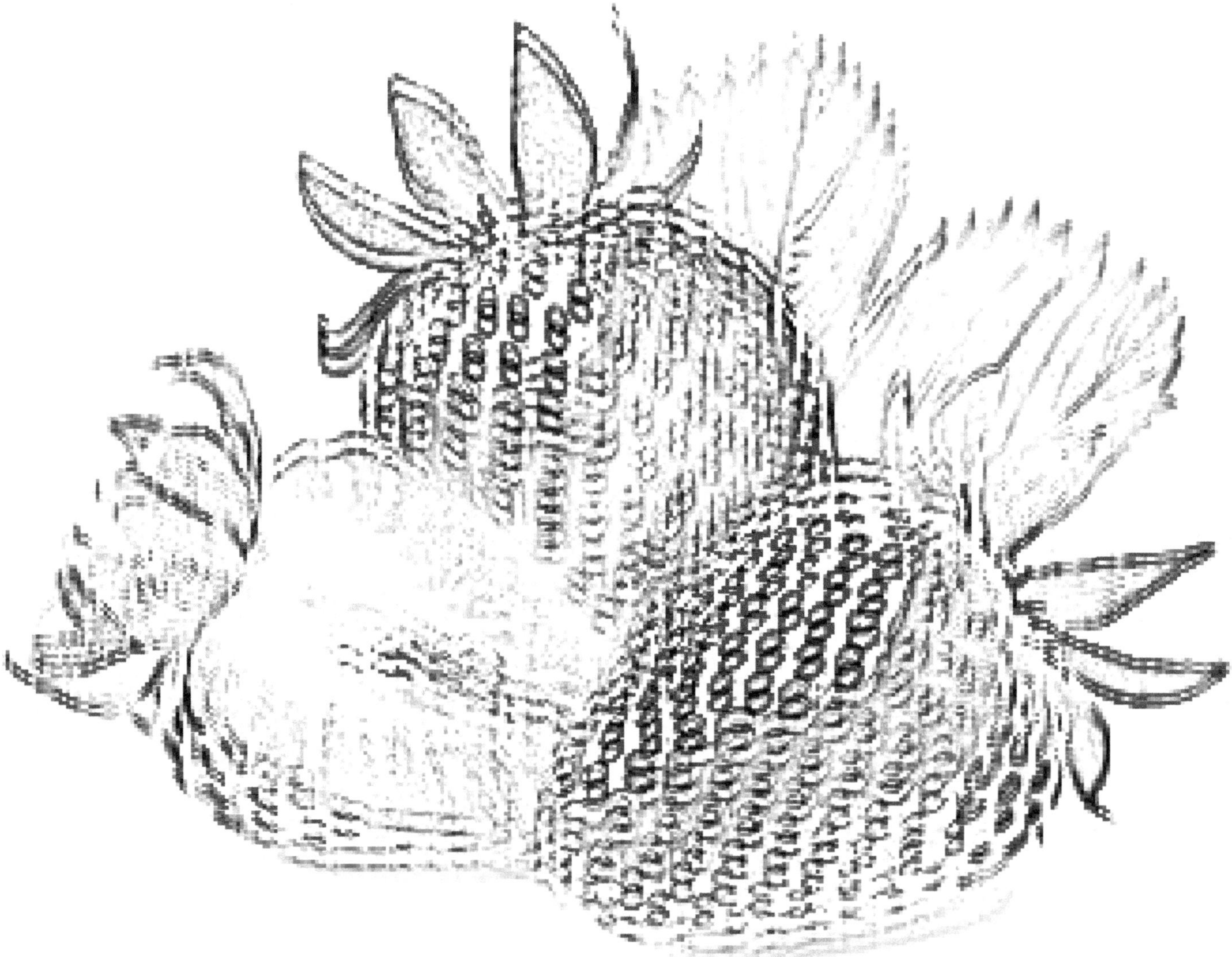

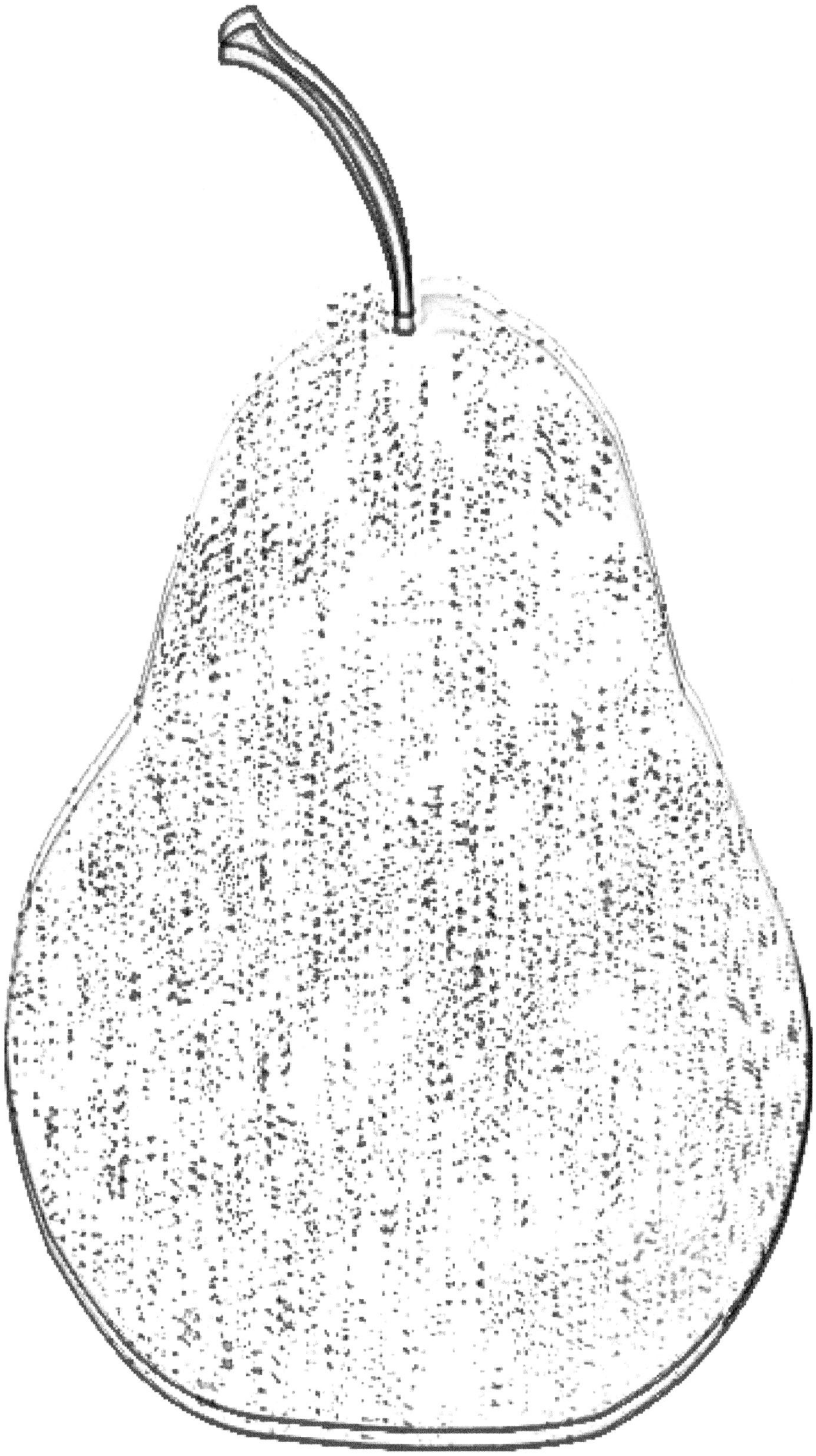

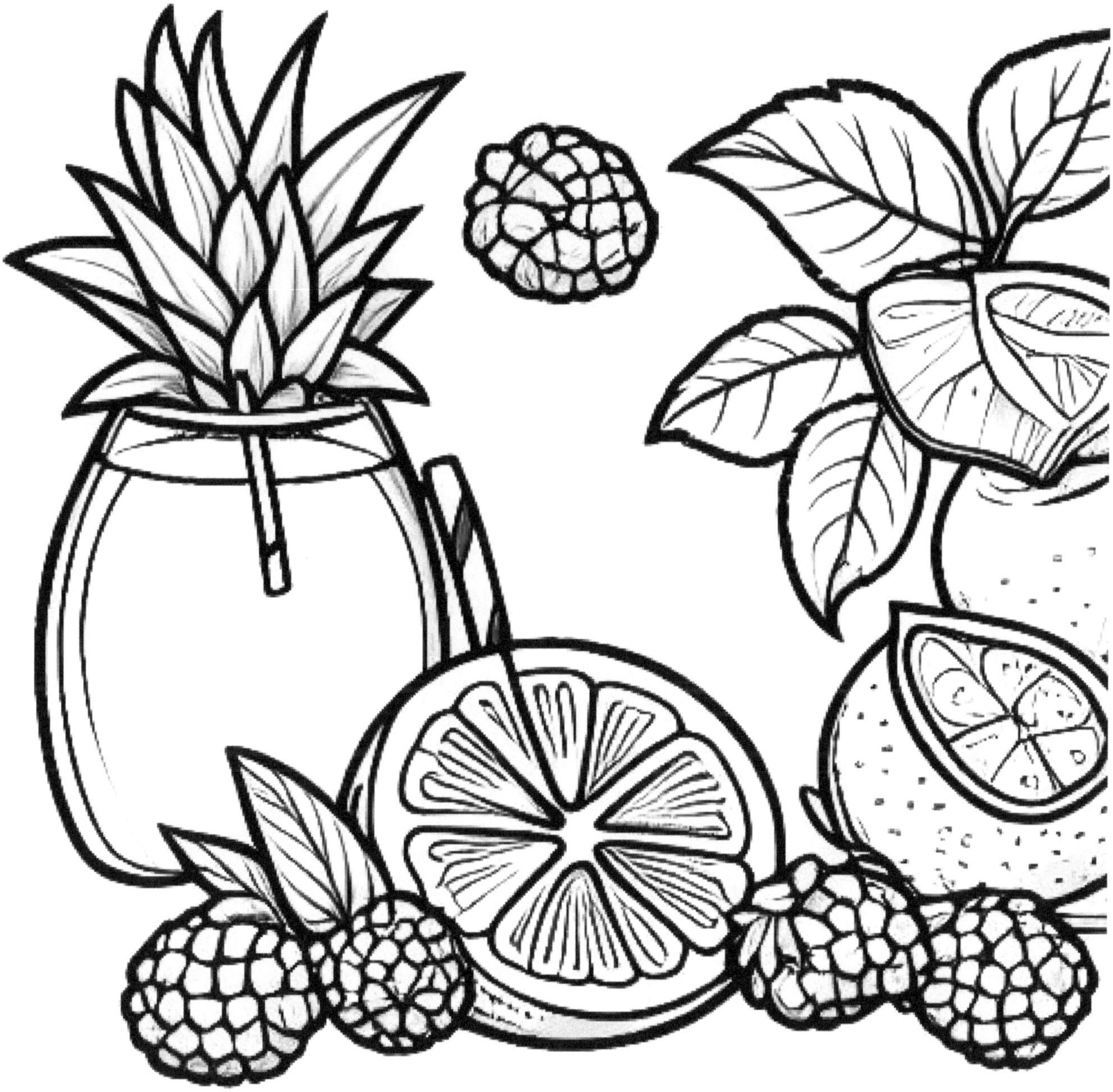

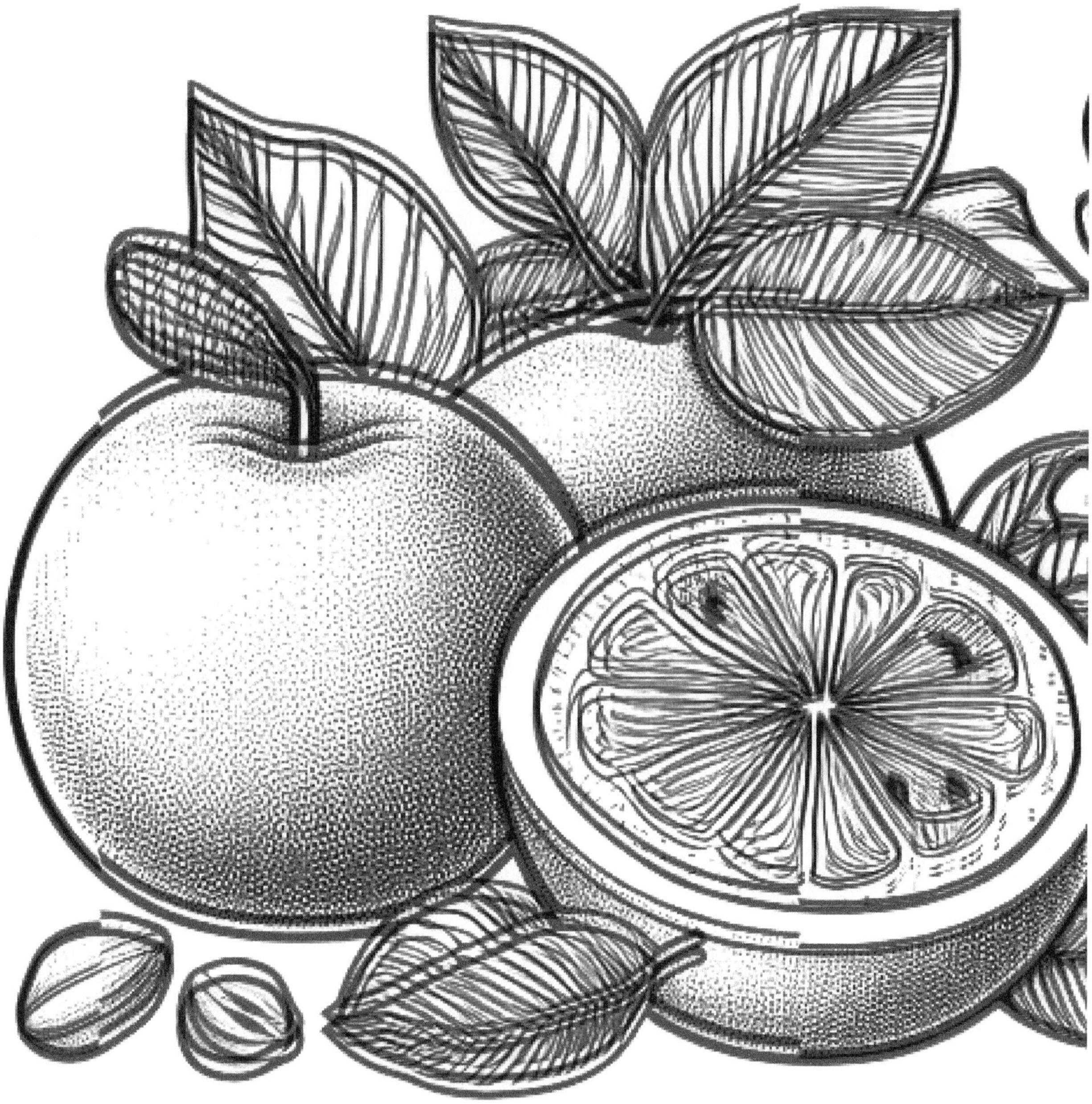

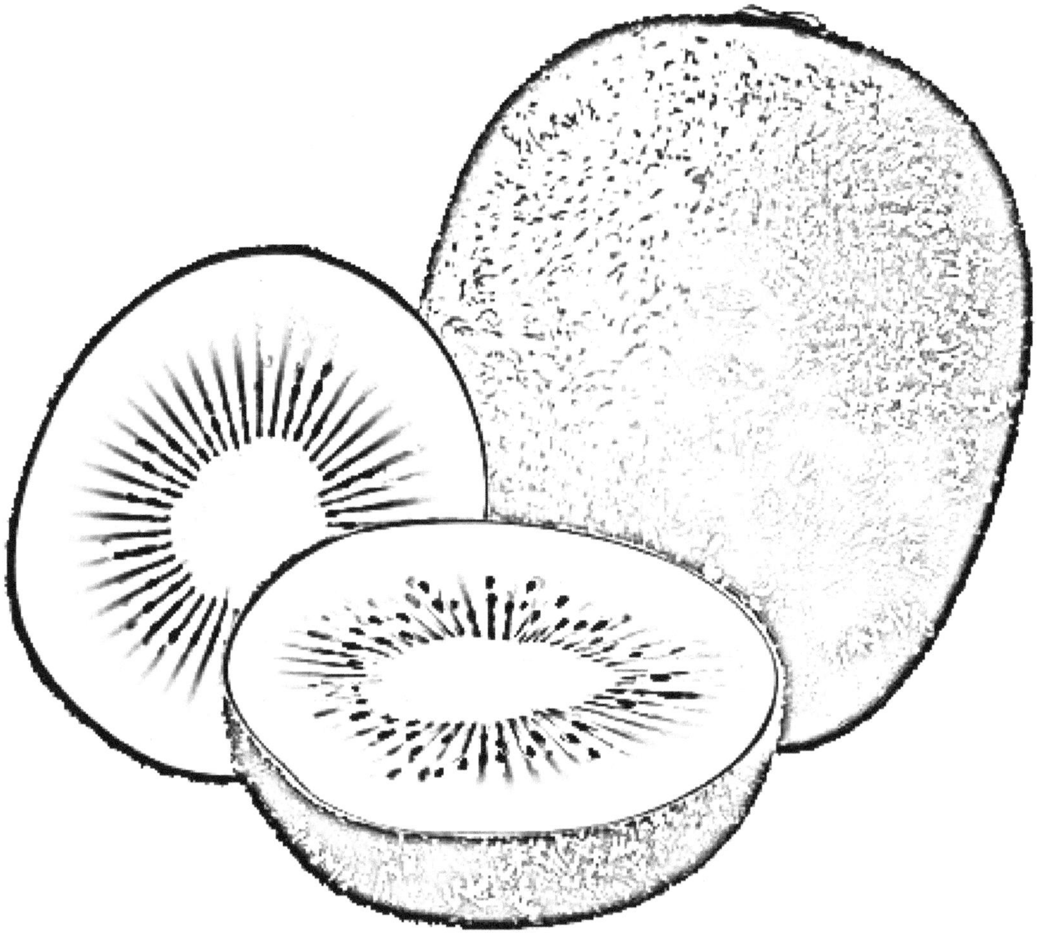

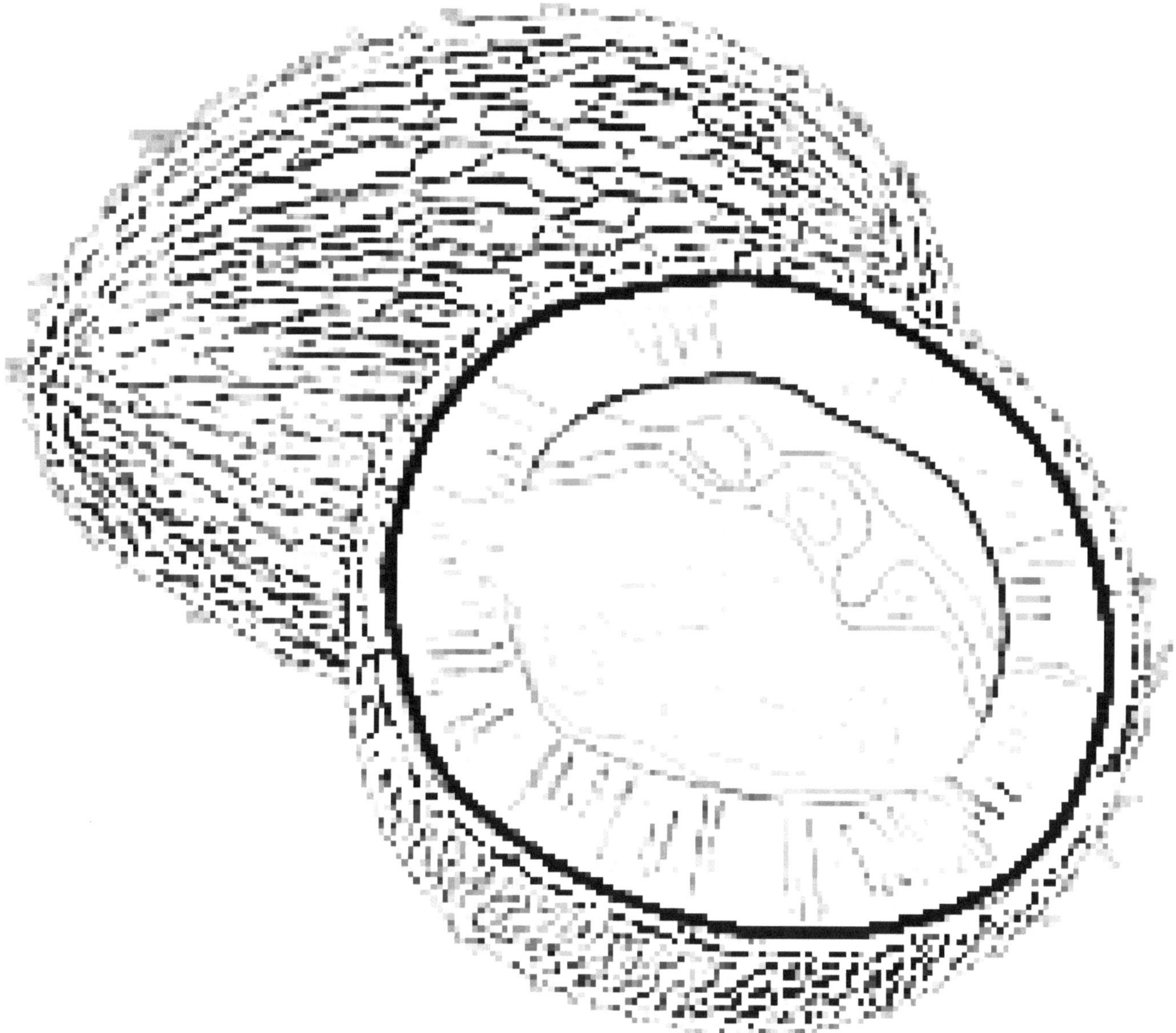

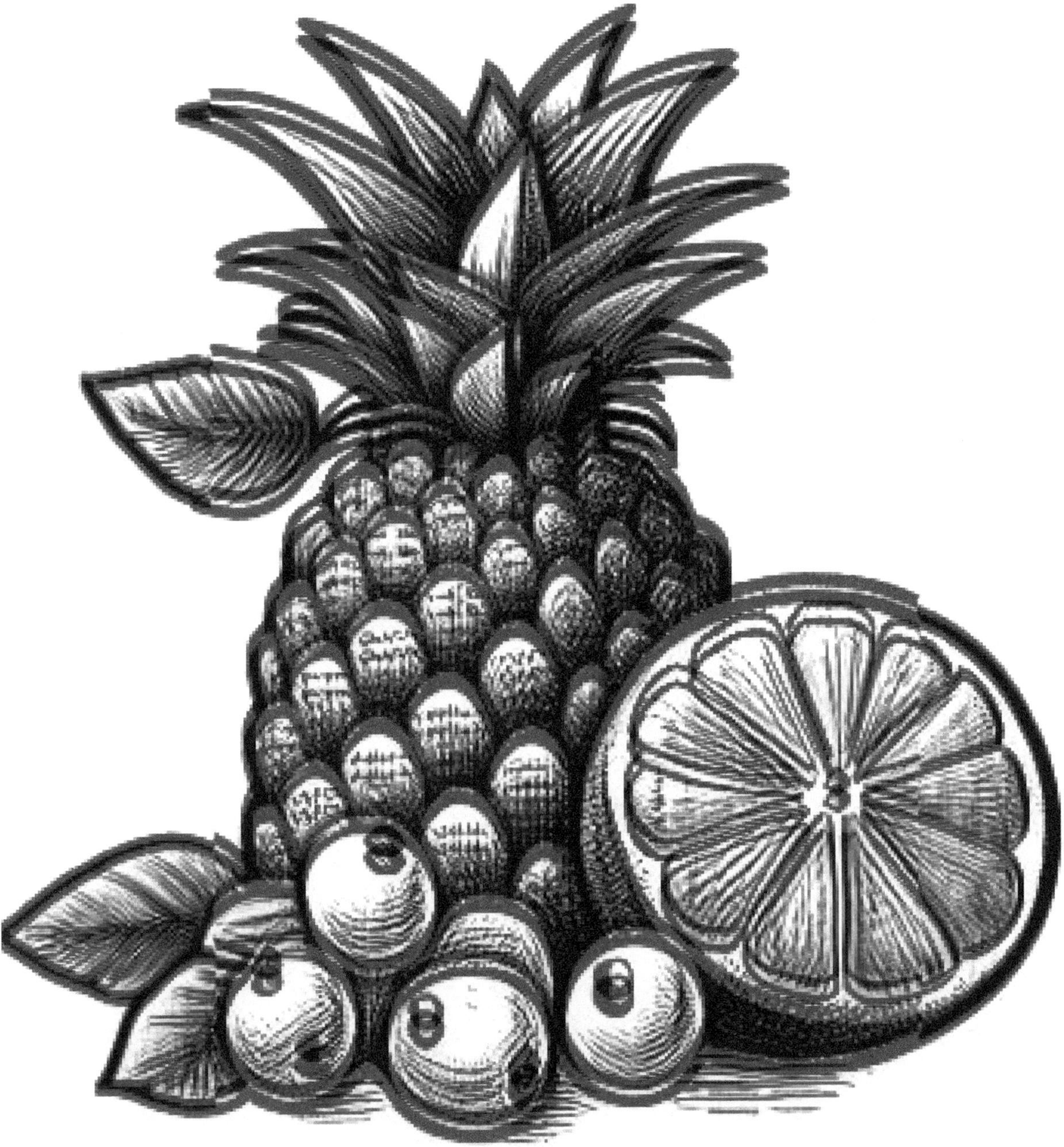

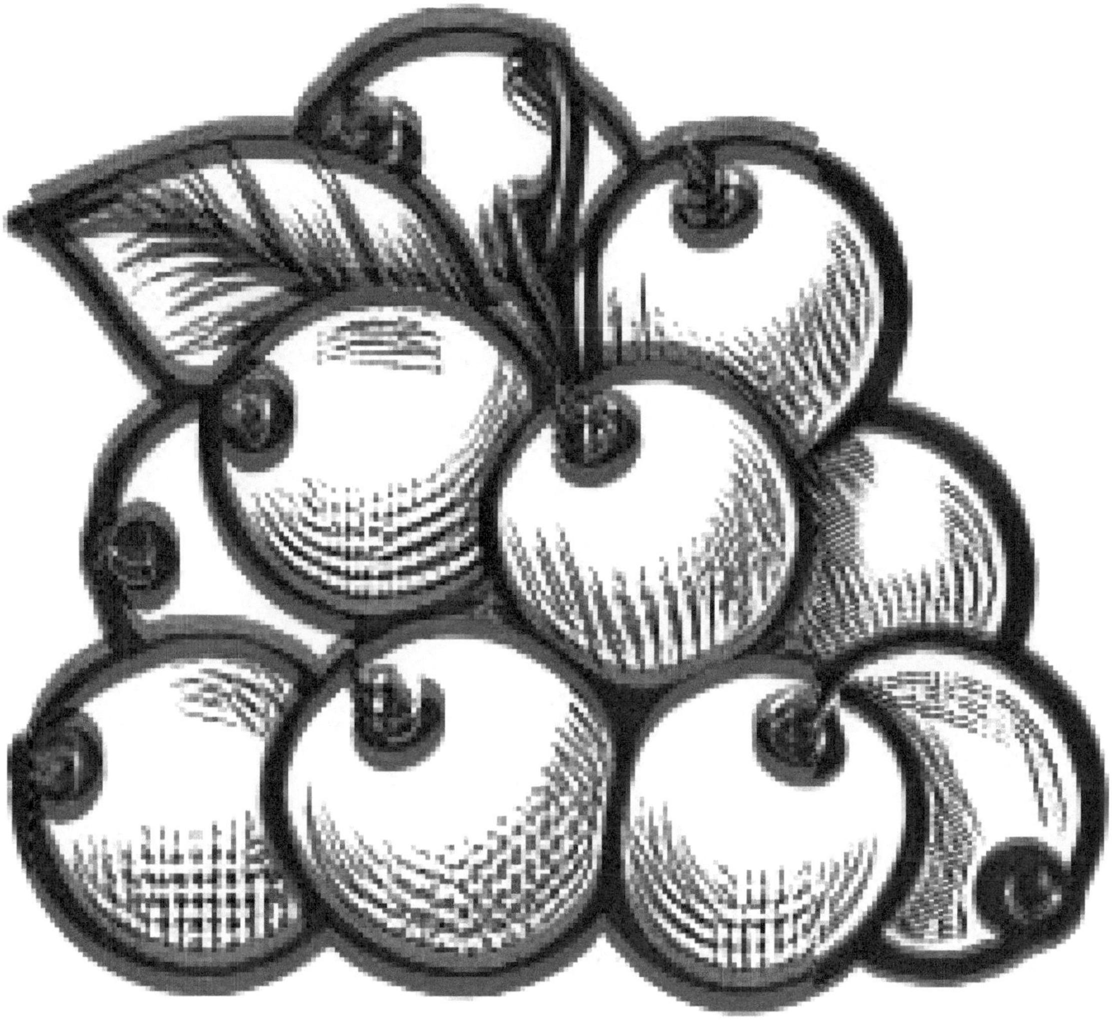

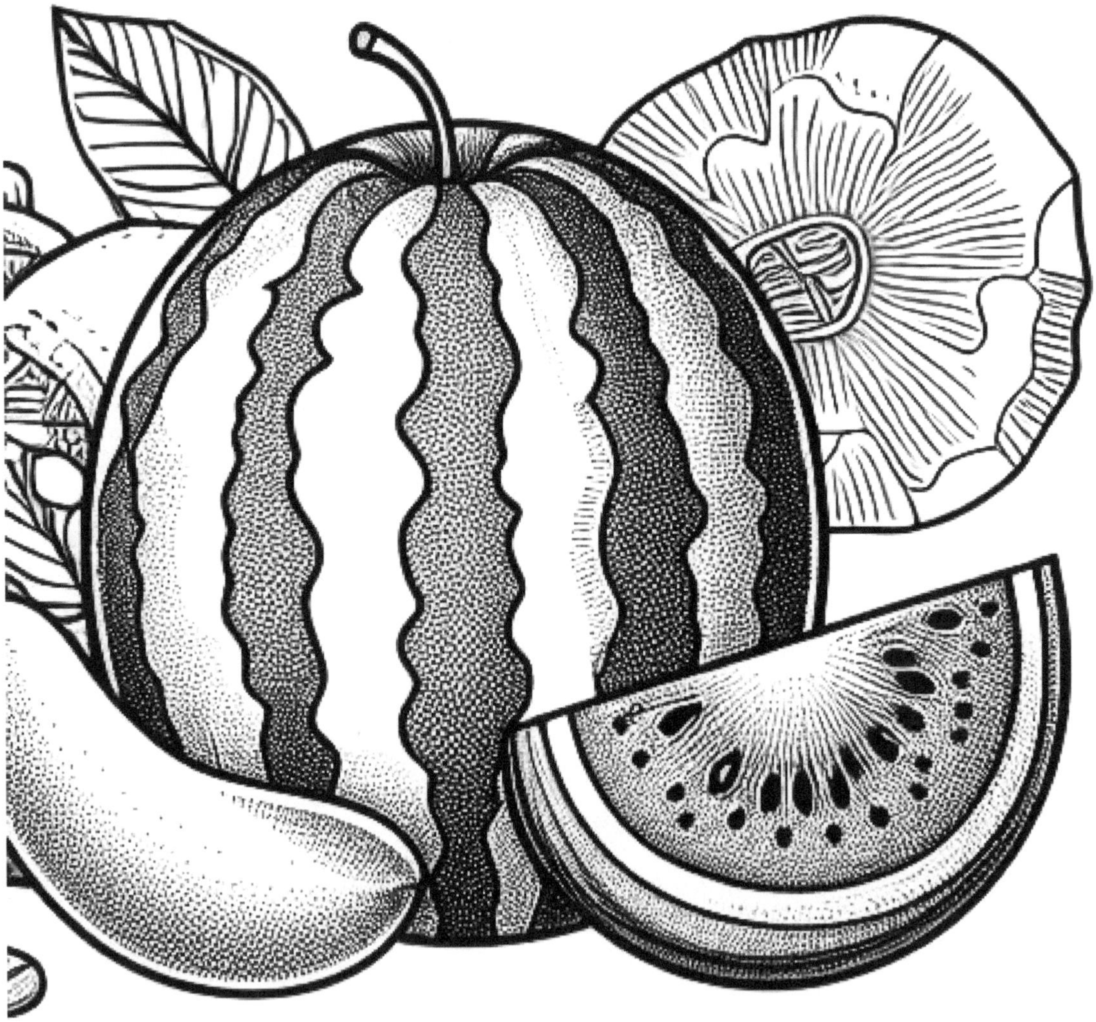

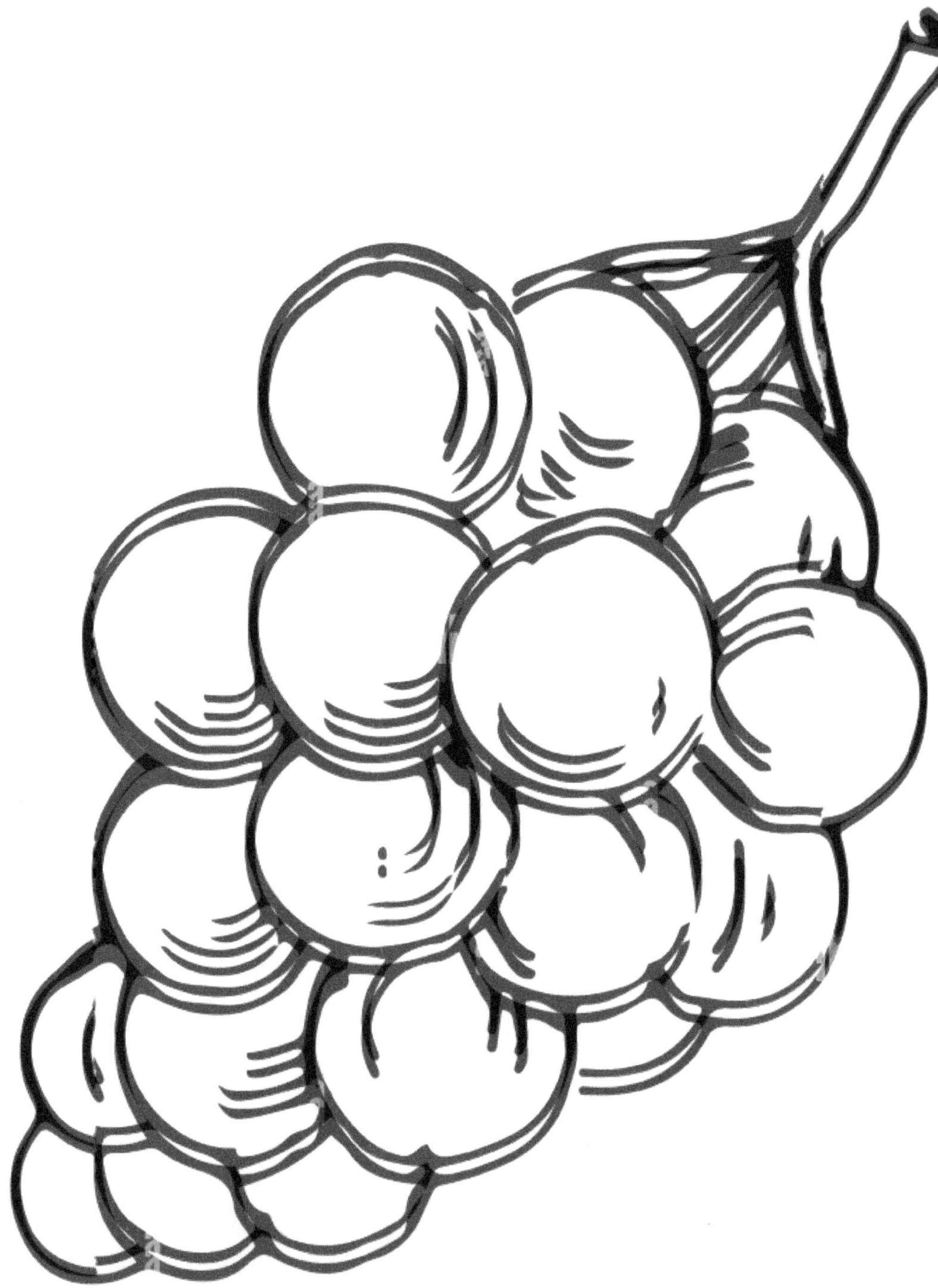

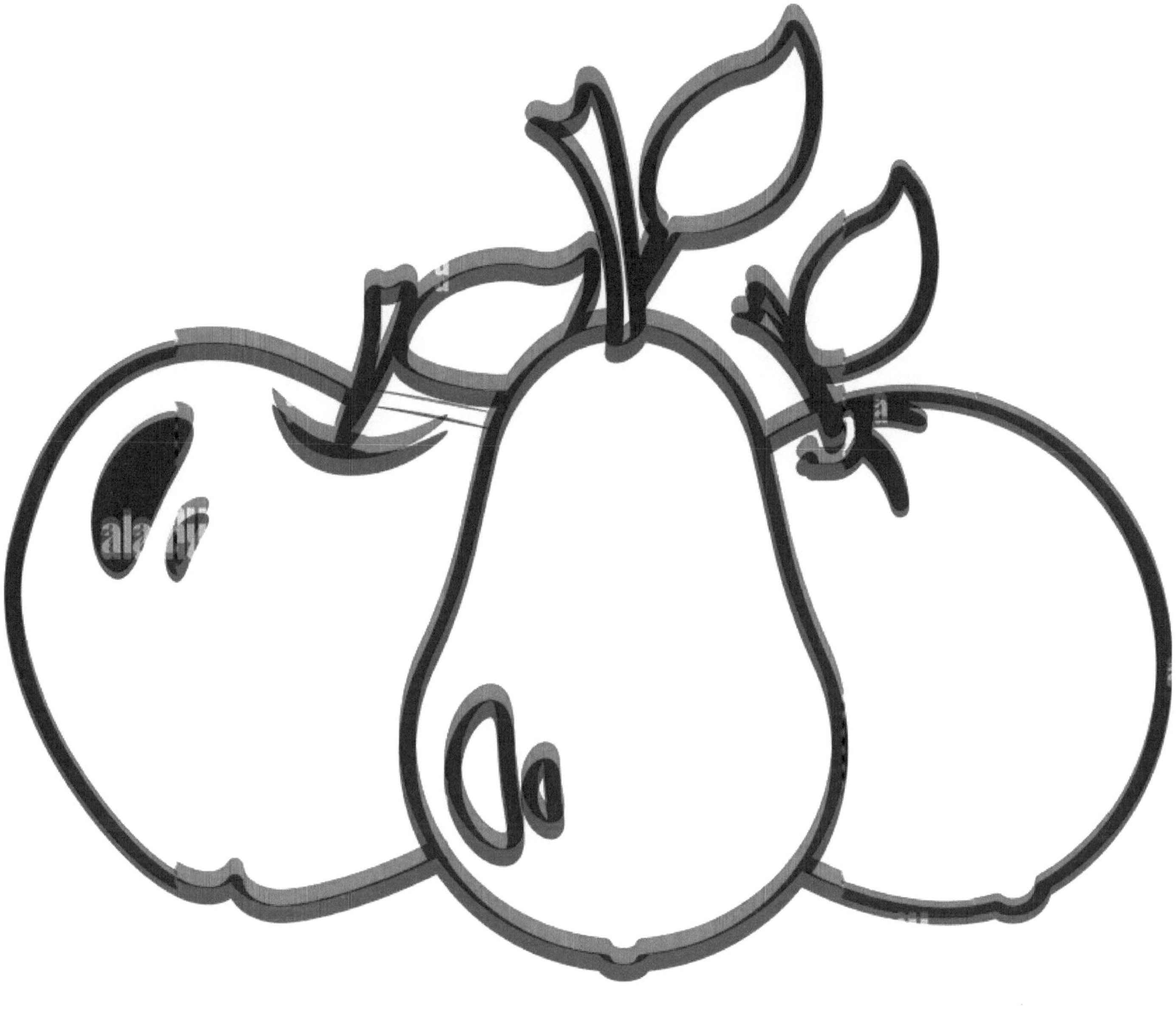

www.ingramcontent.com/pod-product-compliance
Lightning Source LLC
Chambersburg PA
CBHW051937210526
45473CB00006B/2286
9798320361277

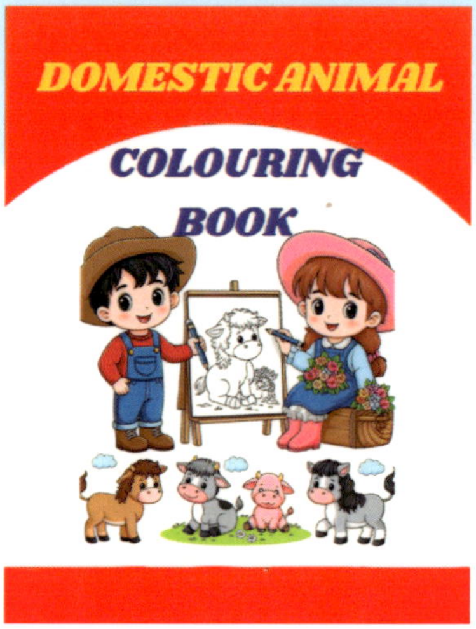

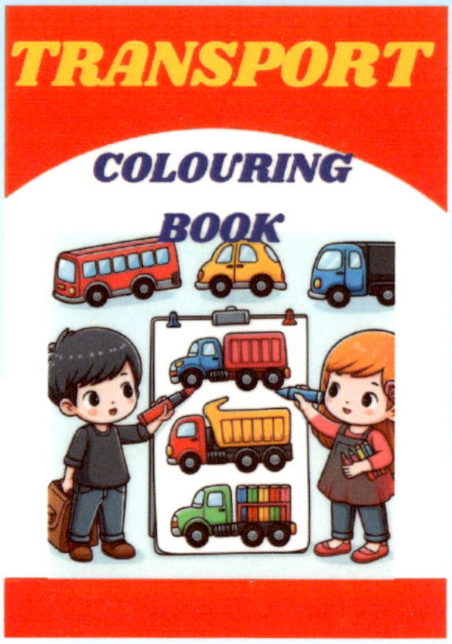

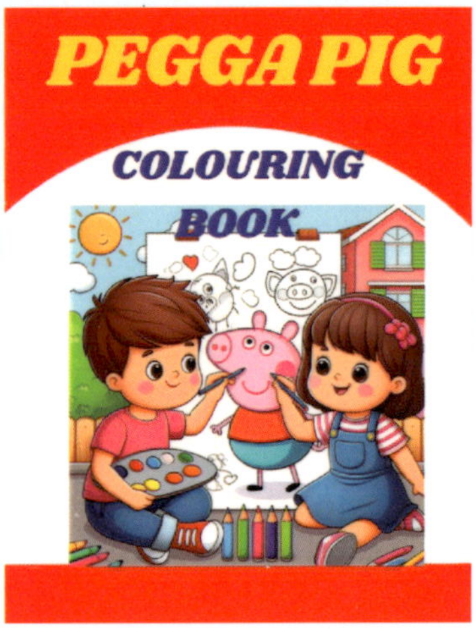

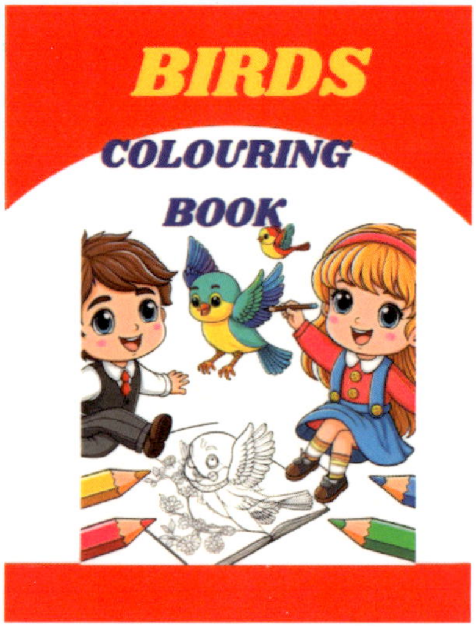

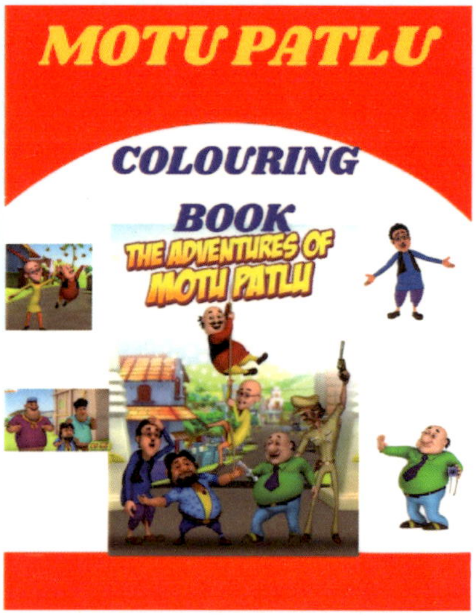

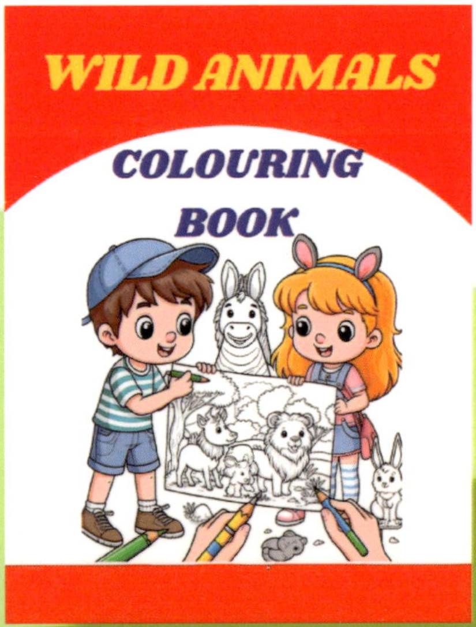

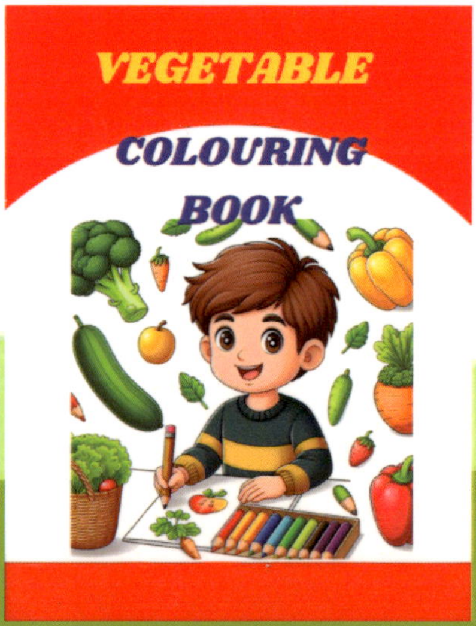

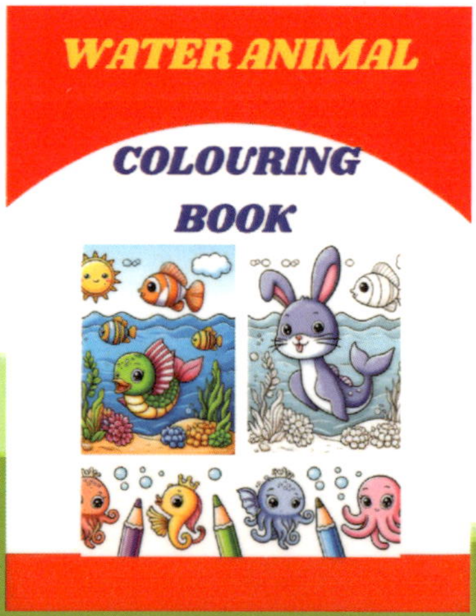

ISBN 9798320361277
90000
9 798320 361277

MATH MADE EASY (NUMBER SENSE)

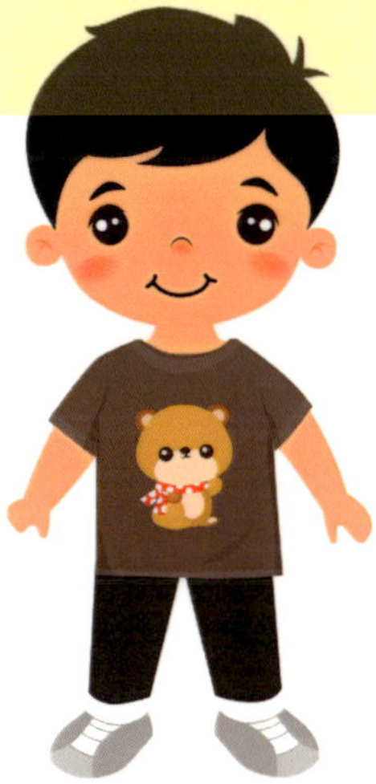

Created with ♥

@learningwithnisha